I07066633

je t'aime

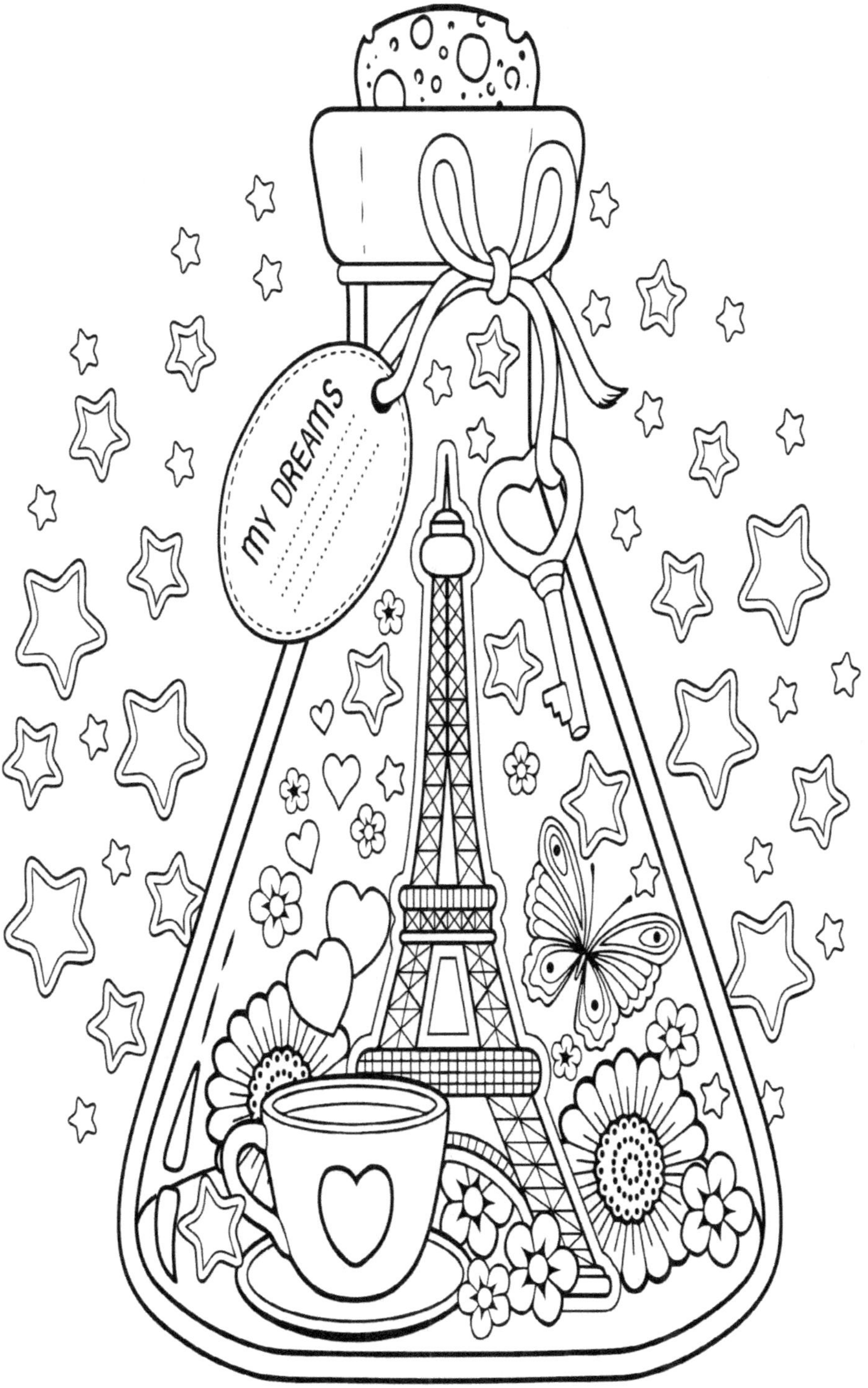
MY DREAMS

XOXO

Я люблю тебя

you are
my
sunshine

Mon Amour

For you

you are the best

you are loved

Ti amo

Be Mine

I love
YOU
to the
moon
AND
back

Love

Ich liebe dich

I love you more than all stars in the sky

To the Best
Mommy
Happy Valentine's
Day!
Coloring
Card

AFGREKI
EU TE AMO
Aishiteru
MILUJI TĚ
T'estimo Je t'aime
Te dua
VOLIM TE
Ľúbim t'a
Te ubesk
I love you
Kocham Ciebie
Ti ama
S'agapo
Mi amas vin
Bahibak
Ich liebe dich
M'bi fe

Copyright 2018 by
Florabella Publishing
All rights reserved. No part of this book may be reproduced in any form or by any electronic means including information storage and retrieval systems without written permissions from the authors.

LOVE
From,